My First Toddler Coloring Book

Fun with Letters , Colors , Animals ,Numbers, and Shapes

A-a

is for

Alligator

B-b

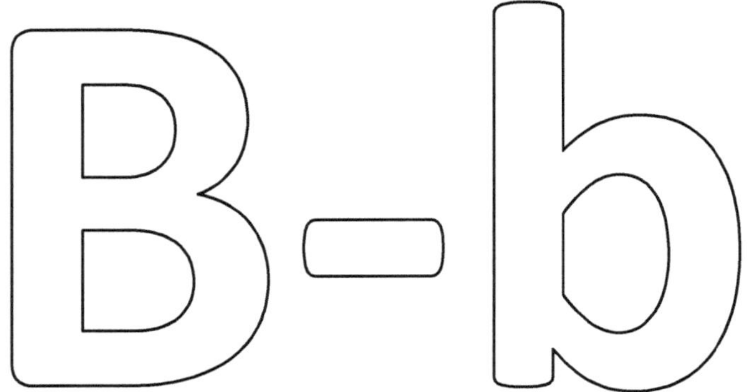

is for

Bee

C-c

is for

Cat

D-d

is for

Dog

Fido

E-e

is for

Elephant

is for

G-g

is for

Giraffe

H-h

is for

Horse

I-i

is for

Iguana

J-j

is for

Jelly fish

K-k

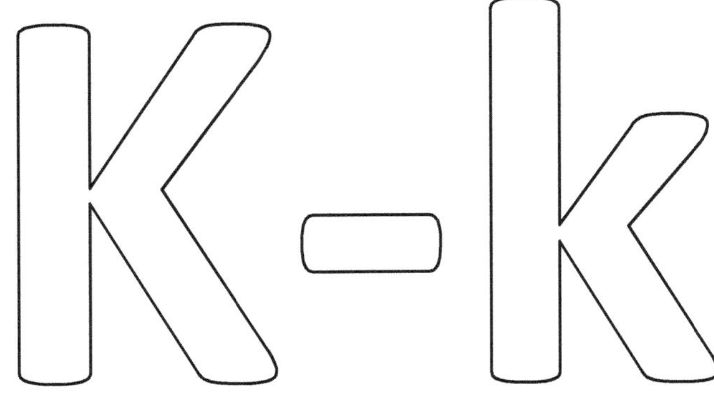

is for

Kangaroo

L-l

is for

Lion

M-m

is for

Monkey

N-n

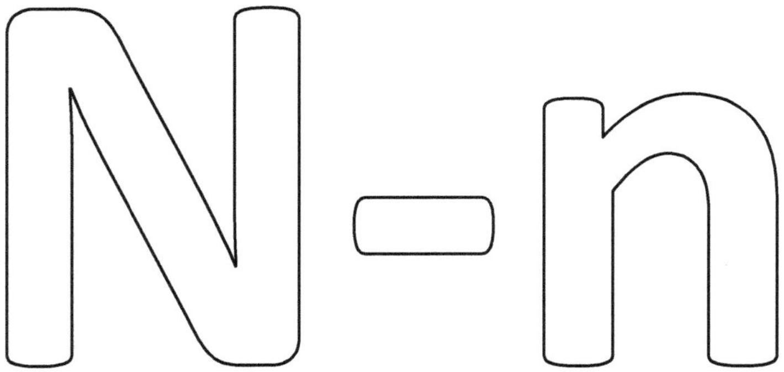

is for

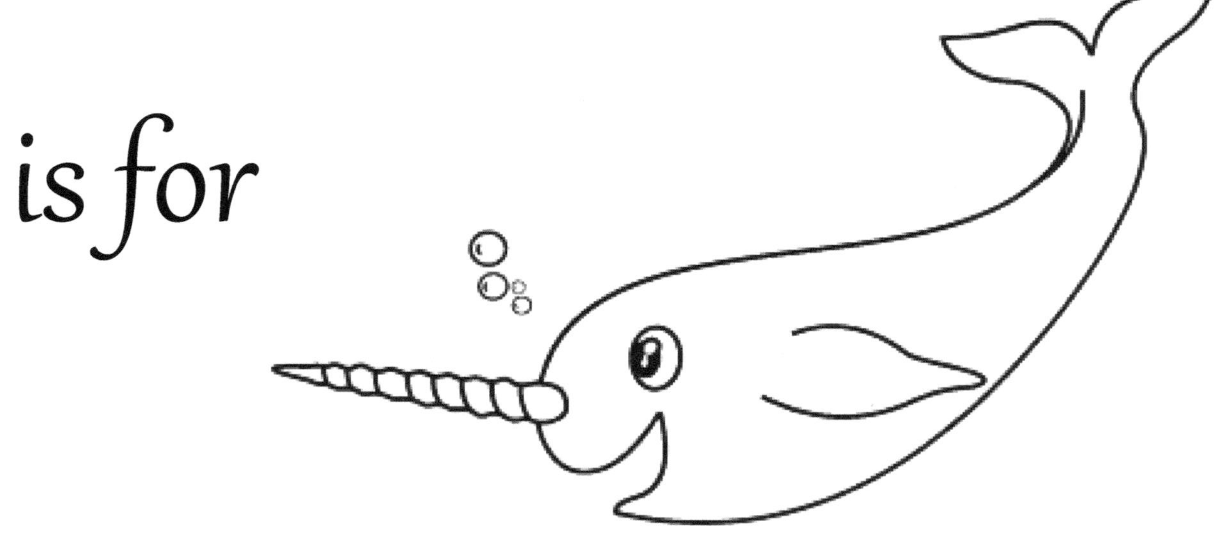

Narwhal

O-o

is for

Owl

P-p

is for

Pig

Q-q

is for

Quail

R-r
is for
Raccon

S-s

is for

Snake

T-t

is for

Tiger

U - u

Upupa

V-v

is for

Vulture

W - W

is for

Walrus

X-x

is for

Xerus

Y - y

is for

Yak

Z-z

is for

Zebra

Numbers

1 2 3

1 ♡

ONE

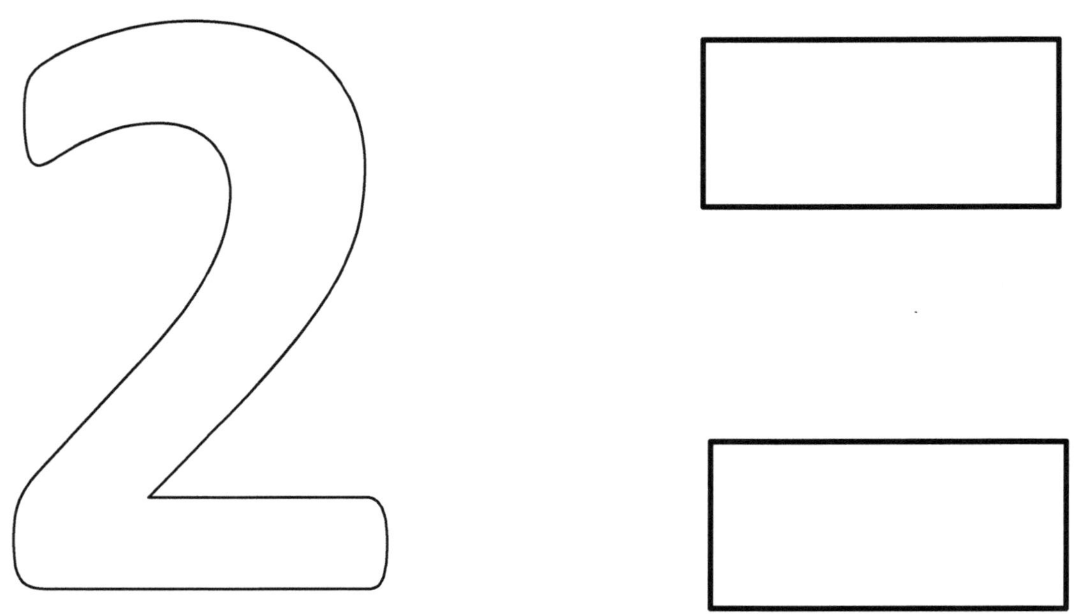

Two

3

Three

4

Four

5

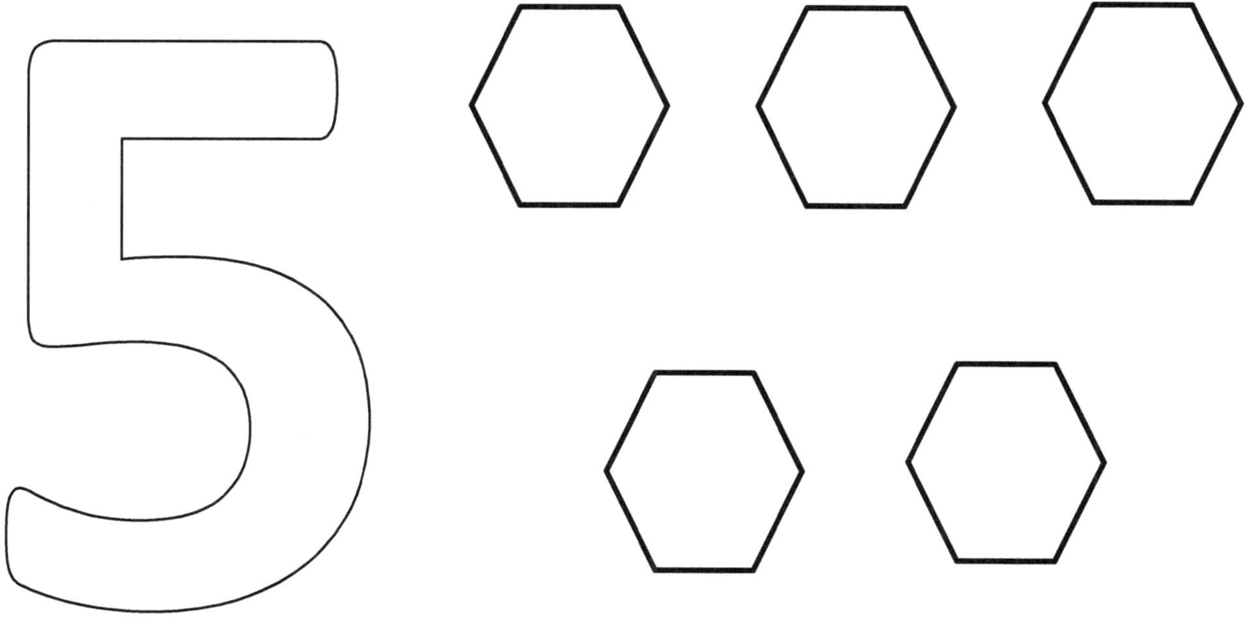

FIVE

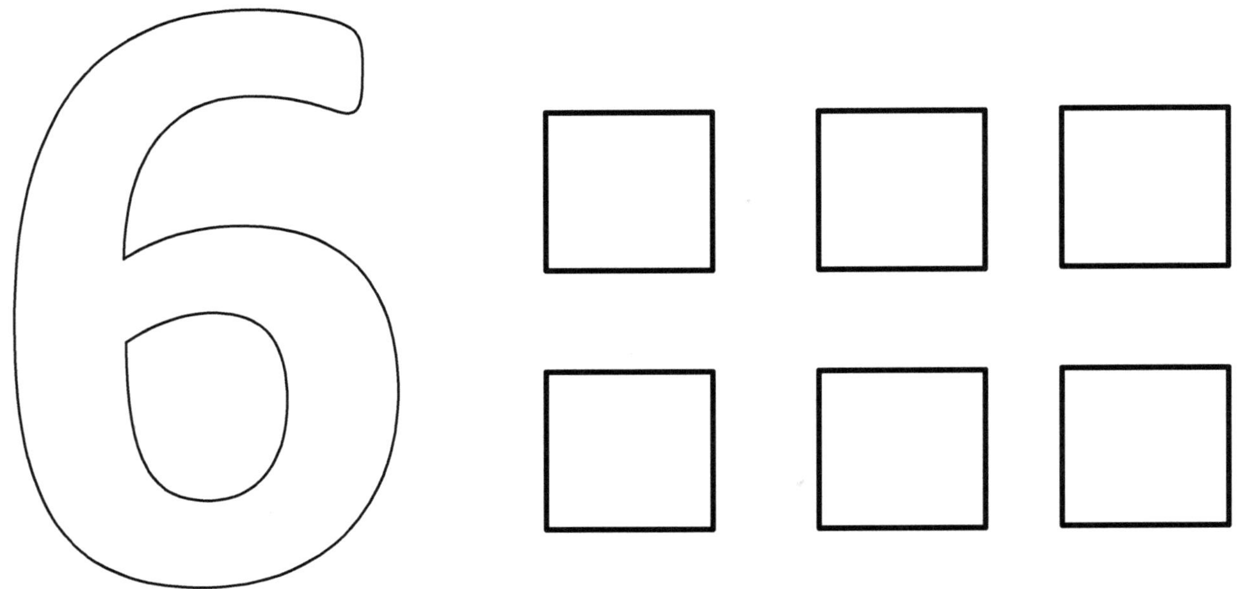

6

Six

7

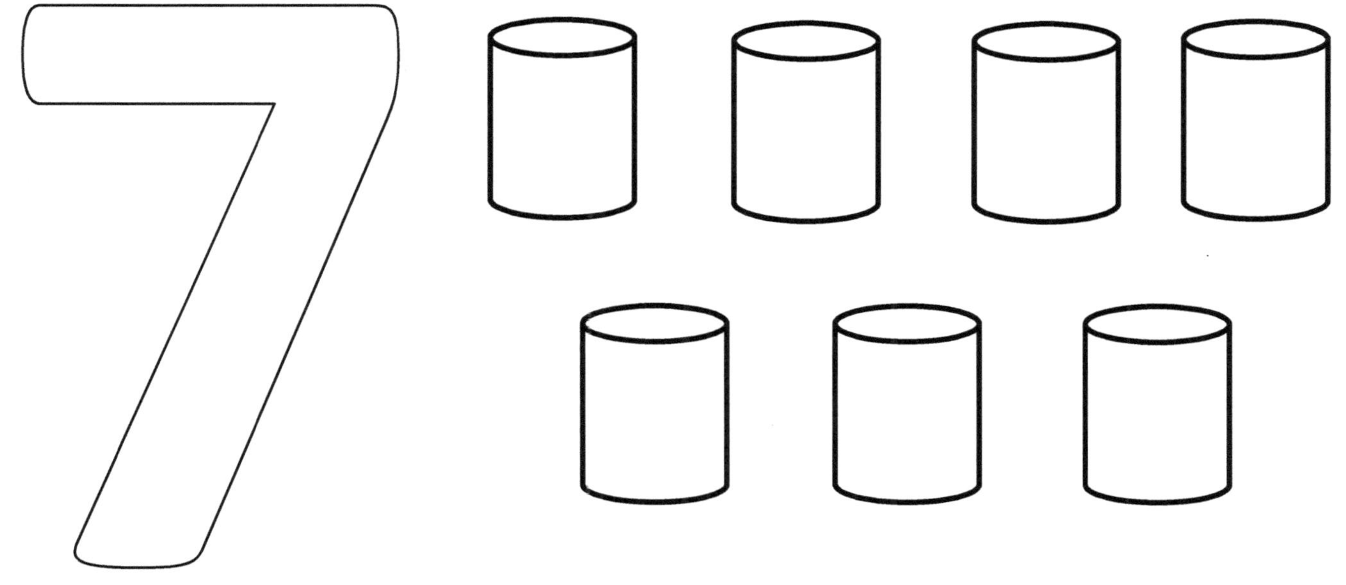

Seven

8

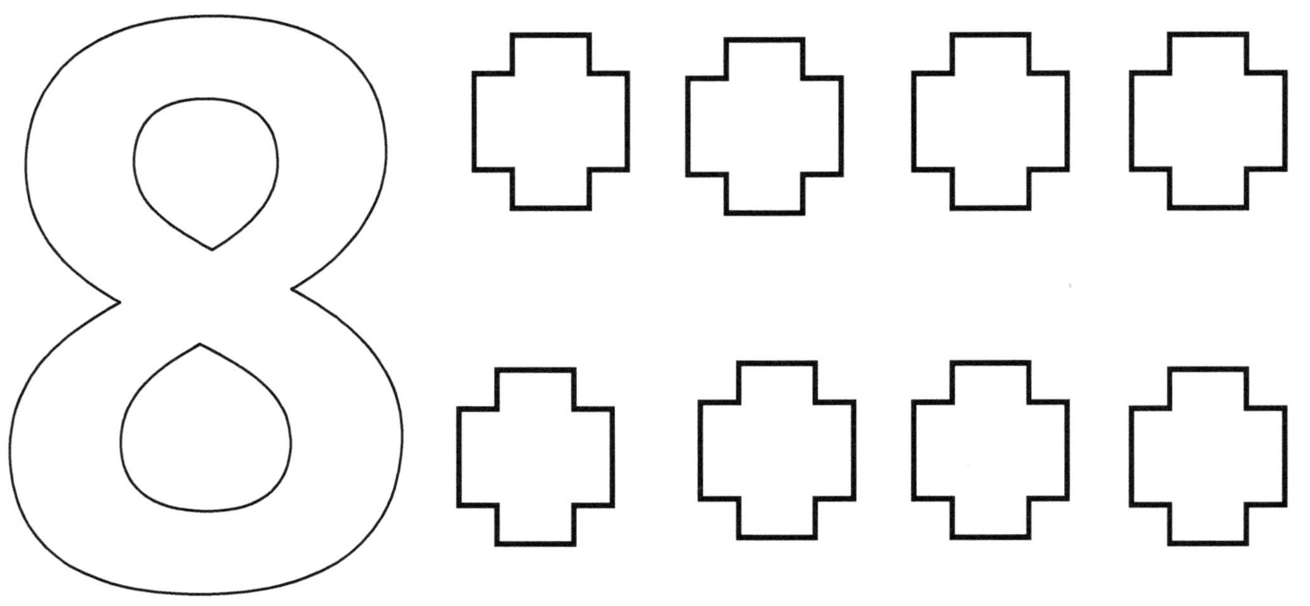

Eight

9

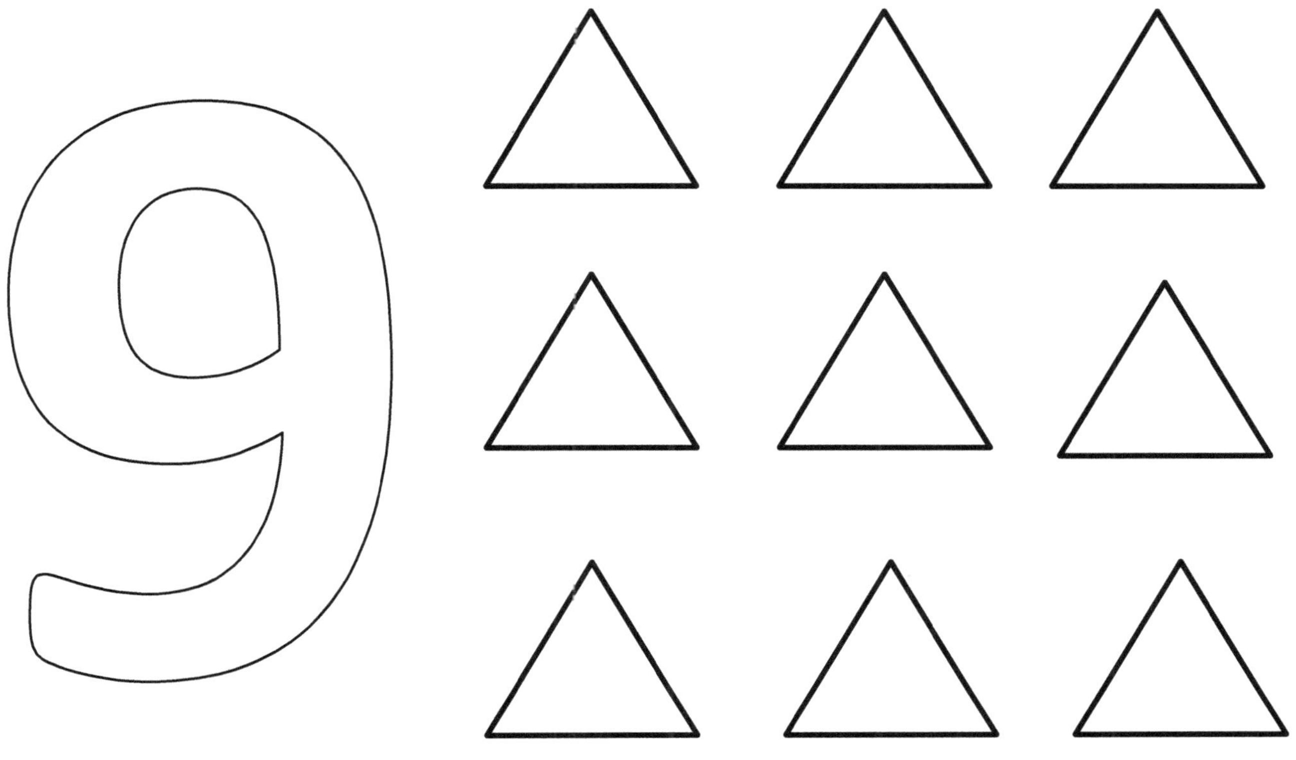

Nine

10

Ten